Negative Thoughts

*Discover How to Stop
Negative Thoughts
by Changing the Way
You Think*

by Anne Seguin

Table of Contents

Introduction

Do you lack hope that anything great will ever happen to you? Are you bothered by the thought of what might happen next, believing that whatever the outcome is, it's not going to be in your favor? Are your memories primarily those of failure, disappointment, or bad news?

If these statements apply to you, then it's time to do something about it.

When negative thoughts inadvertently creep into your head, they tend to quickly find a way of taking over your life. If left to your habitual way of thinking, negative thoughts can have devastating consequences in your life. And knowing such, you have probably tried countless times to stop and force yourself to think about something positive instead, but as you may have found, that's much easier said than done. Negative thoughts are sometimes so strong that they sap our energy and drain our motivation, making us feel physically tired and even sickly.

Having negative thoughts keeps you disconnected to the present moment and when you give in to them, they become even stronger. Swarming around in your head, they are much like tiny snowballs rolling down a hill becoming bigger and bigger and moving faster and faster. One negative thought may turn into a force so strong and fast that it can ruin your day to day life experiences. And what's even worse is that, eventually, the pattern of negative thinking becomes a mental habit that holds you hostage as a prisoner of imagined doom and gloom.

It is difficult, and sometimes even impossible, to get rid of negative thoughts and prevent them from continually reappearing. However, with the guidance from this book, and a little practice, anyone can break free of such negativity.

Once we've identified the root cause of your negative thinking, you'll find that you're much more in control of your thought pattern, and when you're in control, you'll feel less threatened by negativity. And as days go by, you'll notice positive thoughts appearing more and more frequently, without any additional effort on your part. So if this sounds good to you, then please join me along this journey to positivity. By following the tips in this book, you will develop mental strength and emotional calm, and the negativity will fade away completely. Let's get started!

Chapter 1: Understanding What's Really Behind Negativity

Negative thoughts are dangerous things, like a ceaseless enemy that attacks anytime, anywhere. They can easily develop into a habitual way of thinking and eventually squeeze out all those positive thoughts from your mind. When your mind is preoccupied with negative, pessimistic and depressing thoughts, you create a negative energy that goes out into your surroundings and thus creates more negativity and failures.

The way you think determines whether your results will be positive and beneficial or negative and harmful. If you don't believe that you will succeed in doing something, you will unconsciously sabotage your chances to succeed. Similarly, you may be afraid of meeting new people or starting a new relationship, and thus you will find different ways to avoid people and you won't even realize this when you start complaining how nobody loves you and you feel lonely. You will unconsciously give your mind instructions to neglect all the opportunities that come by and therefore will be blind to them.

The reasons for a person's tendency to be overwhelmed by negative thoughts are as plentiful as our varying circumstances. People who grew up in abusive environments are more likely to have a negative outlook in life. They develop the attitude that nothing good ever happens to them and that it is better to expect nothing than be disappointed with life. Another thing that may cause negative thinking is fear, which is not surprising at all because we live in a world where nothing is guaranteed. Some people accept that things are the way they are and it is up to them to try to make the most of circumstances but there are some people who are much too overwhelmed by the fact that almost everything in their lives is not in their control, and that all the things they rely on for their security will sooner or later let them down.

These thoughts, in the long run, could lead to depression, anxiety, even addictions to drugs or alcohol. In other words, when you constantly feel anxious because you think that every mistake you make, no matter how trivial or unimportant it can be, is a big failure, you judge and criticize yourself harshly. Thus, you always feel tense and you find it hard to relax. Depression creeps in when you maintain the belief that you have to be perfect. You set personal expectations that are always too high and not realistic, and when you don't meet them you feel trapped and worthless. Consequently, the depression and anxiety becomes so uncomfortable and overwhelming that you try to find an escape by turning to alcohol or drugs.

Negative thinking sucks out your motivation to pursue your goals and ruins your self-confidence. It prevents you from growing as a person and progressing towards your success. Moreover, it also creates a fear of change. The fear paralyzes you so that you don't see how you can make small steps to your success and at the same time you feel too weak to take the big steps. Negative people think that it is better to just do nothing so as to avoid failure than try to do something.

Challenge these thoughts and as you do, you will gain confidence and be ready to strive to your goals again.

Chapter 2: Recognizing Negative Thinking Patterns

Negative and unproductive thoughts that keep bothering you appear in patterns. Their only purpose is to further contribute to the development of more negative emotions. When you learn how to recognize these patterns, you will be able to make a choice about how you want to react to each. The most common patterns of negative thinking include the following:

CRITICISM

This pattern is related to being critical all the time. You could be extremely critical of yourself, as you don't see your weaknesses and flaws objectively but tend to exaggerate them. Moreover, you somehow fail to see all those great things about you or even when you do notice, you typically minimize them. All of this may lead to a lack of confidence and low self-esteem. People react differently to thoughts of this kind. Some may feel so unworthy that they isolate themselves and never make even a small attempt to achieve their goals whereas others may try to cope with this low self-esteem by trying to attain recognition, status and achievements. Sometimes, you may extend this attitude so that you also appear to be very critical of other people as well.

ANXIOUS THOUGHTS

Negative thoughts can appear in the form of images reflecting your fear that nothing good will ever happen to you. They may also reflect your expectations of bad things that you think are certain to happen. These are not limited to big and important issues, such as your health, family, career, relationships, but can also be caused by ordinary things, such as your car breaking down, for instance. Anxious thoughts appear although there are no indications that they may actually ever come true. You get trapped into this kind of pattern when you start worrying about the future and about everything that could go wrong. This eventually prevents you from progressing towards success.

PROBLEMS

We all have problems, but people who struggle with negative thoughts all the time seem to overlook all the great things that have happened in their lives and instead focus only on their problems. Let's take the example of the car breaking down. To a person with a negative frame of mind, it will preoccupy the mind to such an extent that he will spend days thinking how bad things happen only to him while at the same time he forgets about the things he has going for him, such as a great career, happy family, etc. When you ruminate continuously on your problems and sorrows, you feel depressed, anxious, angry, apathetic, frustrated, and finally you get stuck in negativity.

GUILT

Another pattern of negative thinking develops when you continuously think about the mistakes and bad choices you made in the past. Feelings of worthlessness and guilt then flood you leaving you feeling small. Don't get this wrong, though. Reflecting on your past experiences is one of the ways in which we can mature and learn. But, when you return to these mistakes repeatedly with no intention to learn anything but to criticize yourself, you give way to the creation of a destructive thinking pattern.

NOT HAVING ENOUGH

When you become obsessed with all the things you need to be really happy, you also get caught into another pattern of negative thinking and this pattern is particularly easy to get stuck in. Constant wanting creates feelings of restlessness, discontent and unease. When you always focus on what you need and don't have instead of appreciating what you already have, you create this belief that you are not good enough.

Chapter 3: Learning to Observe Your Own Thoughts

When you are trapped in negativity, it may seem easier to just let it be because you feel you don't have enough energy, strength or motivation to do something and change things for the better. However, your problems won't disappear if you ignore them; on the contrary, your problems will get bigger and those negative thoughts stronger. Here are some strategies that can help you free yourself from the prison of negativity.

AWARENESS

Being aware of your thoughts and paying attention to what is going on in your mind is the foremost way to get rid of negativity. Pay particular attention to patterns of negative thinking mentioned in the previous chapter. Our minds have a tendency to create the same thoughts over and over again. When you are not aware of this, these thoughts get a certain momentum and eventually take control of you. When you consciously bring your attention to these patterns, you become mindful, which enables you to step back and silently observe your thoughts. Once you manage to do this, these negative thoughts will lose the power they have over you.

BE AN IMPARTIAL OBSERVER

When you start observing your thoughts, try to do that impartially. When you look at your thoughts in such a way, you will be objective and see them the way they really are. Not only should you focus on your thoughts but also on your emotions. This may sound strange because you probably want to push all of these away and run off. However, when you learn how to be an impartial witness of your negative thoughts and emotions, you will feel detached from these thought processes and you will develop the ability to stay uninvolved and not get easily carried away by these thoughts. Do you want to know why? Because you'll begin to perceive them as mere objects of your observations.

HERE AND NOW

Most of the time, negative thoughts come from two different sources. The first one is thinking about the past and dwelling on your mistakes, guilt, problems, unfulfilled dreams or expectations. The second source is thinking about the future, which may manifest your fears for yourself, other people or even the whole planet. Or, you may feel stressed out because of your finances, relationships, career, etc. No matter what your thoughts are, your mind needs to go back to your past or travel to the future to create these and when you give in to these thoughts, you become detached from the present moment. To step out of this thinking pattern, try to redirect your attention to the here and now. This is often easier said than done. To do this, first become aware of your environment, i.e. the place you are currently at. Employ all of your senses to get as many details as you can. Don't think about whatever you observe, simply become aware of them and observe them non-judgmentally. Note or observe the scents, sounds, tastes, various sensations that will anchor you to the present moment. When you become fully aware of the present, you will prevent these negative thoughts from arising because the past and future will no longer have any power over your thoughts.

Chapter 4: How to Inundate Yourself with Positivity

BEGIN YOUR DAY WITH POSITIVE QUOTES

Spoken words have a deep effect on people. Your mind reacts in such a way as to keep the words for some time in your memory every time it receives input from these sources: reading and hearing. When you read positive thoughts or quotes aloud, you send a stronger input to your mind and it consequently keeps it longer in your memory. These positive quotes should be the first thing you read when you wake up because they have power to keep you inspired throughout the whole day and remind you to stay positive. You can post quotes that resonate strongly with you on your fridge, at your work place, mirror, or by your bed.

I'M GRATEFUL FOR...

Another way to keep yourself positive is to make a list of things you are grateful for in your life. In that way you will learn to appreciate the things you have now.

SURROUND YOURSELF WITH POSITIVE PEOPLE

When negative thoughts flood your mind, you can't think clearly and your perspective gets a bit distorted. Thus, you should have positive people around you who can give you their perspective on things that keep bothering you.

SING

Next time these negative thoughts start bothering you, sing a song and you'll instantly feel better. Maybe you won't feel like singing but give it a try. You can also try to sing your thoughts. You can use the rhythm of *Row, Row, Row Your Boat*. Your thoughts, no matter how dark they are, will certainly sound silly, absurd and funny and that's the whole point of this practice. You can also say them out loud in a funny voice.

Chapter 5: Practicing Yoga and Meditation

Take up yoga or meditation classes because these will help you learn how to shift your focus. Pushing thoughts away to get firm control over the mind takes time and practice but trying out yoga and meditation techniques may be really helpful. Meditation also helps people melt away anxiety, stress, sadness, etc. Both yoga and meditation will help you stay grounded in the present moment so that instead of letting your thoughts roam to what may happen in the future, you become aware of and appreciate the here-and-now moments.

COLORS AND SOUNDS

Some people respond to particular sounds or images because their minds are easily influenced by certain sensations. If you are one of these people, you can use colors and sounds as your weapon for banishing negative thoughts from your head. You probably have some sound or color that relaxes you, or you even associate certain colors with specific feelings, such as strength, peace and tranquility, joy, etc. So, whenever you feel these negative thoughts creeping in, visualize colors that have a strong effect on you and use them to replace negativity with positivity.

ALLOW YOUR THOUGHTS TO FLOAT AWAY

This has to do with visualizing a big leaf carrying away your worries and negative thoughts. Close your eyes and imagine yourself standing or sitting near a stream or river. There comes a big, green leaf floating. Place one of your worries or thoughts on this leaf and let it float down the river. If there are more thoughts troubling you, imagine more leaves coming and taking your negativity with them.

TELL YOUR THOUGHTS TO MOVE ALONG

Close your eyes and imagine yourself as a sheriff of an old Western town. Give yourself some time to imagine the setting. You are walking down the street and there's an outlaw approaching you and as it draws closer you see that this is one of your negative thoughts. You don't want any trouble and thus encourage this outlaw to calmly walk out of the town, and thus out of your mind. If your negative thoughts keep coming, imagine more outlaws approaching you.

Instead of pushing these thoughts away, acknowledge their existence and release them from your mind.

When they come back again, acknowledge that they have returned and let them go away again. In this way, you gain more control over your thoughts and you also allow new thoughts to enter your mind. You will need some patience with this, but gradually you will teach your mind to let some positive thoughts in.

GO SHOPPING (MENTALLY)

Another trick that may help distract you from this flow of negative thoughts is to visualize yourself in a grocery store. Then imagine yourself standing in front of a shelf in this store and looking at the items on this shelf, paying attention to the exact order of the items. If you don't feel like shopping, you can go with anything else that requires concentration. For instance, you can imagine or try to remember the exact order of songs in your favorite playlist, the order of books on your bookshelf, etc. You can do this for a minute or two but it is important to do it whenever you feel negative thoughts coming back at you. If that means that you will do this every 10 minutes, it's perfectly fine. Eventually, your mind will be trained to go in the opposite direction when these thoughts start appearing.

Chapter 6: How to Effectively Introduce Positive Thoughts

When you begin to introduce positive thoughts to your internal conversations, it may sound or appear strange because your mind was used to a negative thinking mode. However, new positive thoughts may lead you to solutions you were not able to notice before and thus turn your problems and obstacles into opportunities. Here are a few ways to shake your thoughts and think positively:

WHAT IS THE OPPOSITE OF THIS?

Any thought can be transformed into a positive one. Whenever you are faced with a challenge, bad circumstance or negative thought, transform these into their opposites. Instead of thinking about how you don't have enough strength to fight all these challenges, think about its opposite: what strength can you use to befriend the challenge. If you visualize failure, know its opposite is triumph and you have the ability to visualize that instead. Notice how you use negative words in your conversations, and mindfully train yourself to switch to positive ones.

CHOOSE CONSTRUCTIVE THOUGHTS

As you develop inner awareness, you can also choose to change your negative thoughts which are destructive into positive and constructive ones. These can help you face daily situations in a practical and effective way. Moreover, just as negative thoughts prevent you from acting, constructive thinking encourages you to take action and deal with any problem that may arise.

CAN ANYTHING GOOD COME OUT OF THIS?

Try to find positive and useful information in difficult situations to help you stay encouraged to move on. Let's say you are going through a difficult financial period and so it's no surprise that your mind is flooded with myriad negative thoughts. However, you can certainly find something positive in this. For instance, you learned to manage your money better and maybe even found some ways to invest your money wisely. So, whenever you find yourself in a situation which is likely to spark your negative thinking, try to reframe the event in your mind. Stuck on a bus because of a traffic jam? Be thankful for the time to call a friend or your parents, read a book, listen to your favorite song, etc.

Chapter 7: Changing Your Mindset – What to Avoid

DON'T THINK IN EXTREMES

Nothing in life is black or white. When you think like this, you miss out the very many nuances between these two extremes. Consequently, you see the future as filled with failures, dramatic events and catastrophes. The truth is that black moments sometimes come in everyone's life while most times we experience grey moments. Instead of thinking of how your business plan will leave you ruined, think about how it will take some time to get going.

Although most will say that negative thoughts can be overcome once one starts to think positively, you can't be positive all of a sudden. Instead try to look for those grey moments that are hiding almost everywhere. Another way to get this right is to write down some of your negative thoughts and then write their corresponding extremes. Then, write the possibilities in the middle grey that are actually the most numerous and have greater chances of occurring.

DON'T TAKE ALL THE RESPONSIBILITY

Negative thinkers react in two different ways when it comes to responsibility. In one way, they tend to internalize the negative, which means that they blame themselves both for the things that have to do with them and things that actually aren't related to them or within their control at all. So, first consider how much influence and control you have over certain things before you take any responsibility for them. On the other hand, these people also tend to externalize the positive. This means that they don't take credit for something good they have done. It may also appear that when someone does something kind, negative thinkers believe that it was done only because of some ulterior motive. Simply learn how to accept when other people or you do something great.

DON'T WALLOW IN VICTIM MODE

When you think of yourself as a victim, you will find reasons and justifications for all those negative thoughts and believe they are all true. Don't permit yourself to waste your inherent ability and strength to choose your thoughts and get rid of any thoughts that aren't helping you. You are not benefitting from victim mode. So, acknowledge the things that have happened to you, find the right reasons why they did and decide that from now on you are to make informed choices.

DON'T FORGET—NO ONE IS PERFECT

Sometimes, it can be tempting to repeatedly replay the mistakes you have made in your mind, but this will lead you nowhere. Instead, deliberately choose to spend this time differently, remembering that we are not perfect beings. No one is, not even the biggest names in business or hot shot celebrities, though at first glance they appear to be perfect and their lives glamorous. They are just like you and me: they have their own flaws, problems, and troubles.

DON'T OVER-GENERALIZE THE NEGATIVE

When you experience something bad, don't turn that experience into a general statement that applies to everything. For example, if you fail a test, accept that you failed that one test, and stop yourself from saying you are bad at taking tests in general, or worse that you are no good or dumb. Even the best chefs sometimes whip up what turns out to be a lousy dish, but it would be wrong to let that one meal define him as a chef, wouldn't it?

Instead of berating yourself, think about how you can and will do better next time. This also means that when you experience something positive, you will probably fail to see it that way. So, don't minimize the positive either. The key to this is to see all the setbacks not as permanent but as temporary things that come and go.

DON'T GO LOOKING FOR NEGATIVES

Negative thoughts prevent you from relaxing or creating and instead fill you with uncertainty. Consequently, this leads to mindreading, i.e. analyzing other people's words and attributing certain meanings to what they say which is almost always not their intent.

For instance, you may be waiting for a reply to a message you have sent a friend, and if you don't get one in an hour, you start analyzing this and drawing various conclusions, often false ones. (Maybe she is angry with me or thinks my time is not important.) You assign meanings to things or situations even without evidence. Do this often enough and you will tend to believe in these imagined meanings and overlook the ones you have evidence for. Learning to dismiss ungrounded thoughts and postponing conclusions is essential in overcoming negative thinking. Once you manage this, you will see how your thoughts about the same situation can be changed as well. Also, you will learn to consider all the possible reasons for any given situation and not just the negative ones.

DON'T USE YOUR IMAGINATION TO SCARE YOURSELF

Use imagination constructively. Some of us create images of the worst things that may happen and end up scaring ourselves silly with these vivid images. Instead, try to use your imagination in a constructive way. Imagine things going well and try to simulate how good you will feel when things turn out the way you want. This will help you feel calm and prepared if you ever find yourself in this situation. It may be hard at first, especially if your negative images are too strong, but keep at imagining several different positive outcomes and you will find it gets easier.

DON'T MAKE UP RULES

Sometimes negative feelings may lead you to create certain rules about what reality should be like which will lead you to have certain expectations based on these rules. You might say life is never fair or good people always get cheated on. Rules like these are too tight, unreasonably inflexible and don't reflect the true nature of reality. Next time you get disappointed, don't fall back to these rules to explain your disappointment, but challenge and ask yourself why your expectations were too narrow or unrealistic.

Conclusion

Overcoming negative thoughts is actually based on realizing that these thoughts sometimes bother even the most positive people you know. What makes the difference for positive, productive people is the way in which they allow these thoughts to manifest and influence their everyday life.

Give the techniques in this book a try and see how negative thoughts gradually start to disappear from your mind as you strengthen your will and mental discipline (which will greatly help other aspects of your life too). The more time you spend trying to apply these tips in different situations, the faster you will be able to get rid of negative thoughts. Eventually, these habits of mind will become weaker and you will be able to live your life to the fullest again.

Finally, I'd like to thank you for purchasing this book! If you enjoyed it or found it helpful, I'd greatly appreciate it if you'd take a moment to leave a review on Amazon. Thank you!